FAVORITE
BIBLE FAMILIES
Ages 2 & 3

rainbowpublishers®

Rainbow Publishers • P.O. Box 261129 • San Diego, CA 92196
www.RainbowPublishers.com

FAVORITE BIBLE FAMILIES

Ages 2 & 3

Bonnie Line

To Scott Howard and Nicholas: May Jesus be the love of your lives! Love, Grandma

FAVORITE BIBLE FAMILIES FOR AGES 2 & 3
©2010 by Rainbow Publishers, first printing
ISBN 10: 1-58411-022-8
ISBN 13: 978-1-58411-022-4
Rainbow reorder# RB38051
RELIGION / Christian Ministry / Children

Rainbow Publishers
P.O. Box 261129
San Diego, CA 92196
www.RainbowPublishers.com

Cover Illustrator: Court Patton
Interior Illustrator: Ron Forkner

Scriptures are from the *Holy Bible: New International Version* (North American Edition), ©1973, 1978, 1984 by the International Bible Society. Used by permission of Zondervan Bible Publishers.

Printed in the United States of America

Contents

Introduction

We are all a part of some family, whether it is a family with parents and children, a family with a spouse, a larger extended family or God's family of believers. In the Bible, there were many different types of families. Some obeyed God, while others did not. Yet they are all important because we can learn from them how to live as a family and as Christians.

God has a purpose for each family. As a teacher, you have the awesome responsibility of introducing your students to how God uses families in the Bible and in today's lives. Two- and three-year-olds are just becoming aware of relationships within their own families. The activities in *Favorite Bible Families for Ages 2&3* are designed for identifying roles in families, explaining God's plan for families and instructing children about the consequences of obeying and disobeying God.

Each Bible family in this book is a lesson unit, with several themes that apply to the family. Suggestions for directed conversations with your children are contained in the "What to Say" section of each lesson. A materials list and step-by-step instructions will help you make the most of your lesson time. To minimize material costs, send home the reproducible Note to Families on page 9.

In the last chapter of the book, there are lessons for the Family of God. These four lessons explain the steps to receive Christ as Savior; it is never too early for kids to learn about God's salvation plan. And other family members may read the take-home lesson page and learn how they too can be a part of God's family!

TO FAMILIES OF TWO- AND THREE-YEAR-OLDS

We have some exciting activities planned for use in teaching Bible lessons this year. Some of these crafts use ordinary household items. We would like your help in saving these items for our activities.

❏ cotton balls   ❏ ribbon, ¼"

❏ craft sticks, 6" size   ❏ sequins, large and small flat

❏ fake fur   ❏ yarn

❏ leather strips, small

❏ magazines

❏ magnets

❏ paper plates, large and dessert size

Please bring the items on _____.

Thank you for your help!

_____
Teacher

TO FAMILIES OF TWO- AND THREE-YEAR-OLDS

We have some exciting activities planned for use in teaching Bible lessons this year. Some of these crafts use ordinary household items. We would like your help in saving these items for our activities.

❏ cotton balls   ❏ ribbon, ¼"

❏ craft sticks, 6" size   ❏ sequins, large and small flat

❏ fake fur   ❏ yarn

❏ leather strips, small

❏ magazines

❏ magnets

❏ paper plates, large and dessert size

Please bring the items on _____.

Thank you for your help!

_____
Teacher

Memory Verse Index

Adam and Eve's Family
I Am Special

Memory Verse
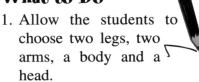

God created man.
~ Genesis 1:27

Before Class

Duplicate the body parts on various colors of paper and cut them out, at least one set per child (cut two arms and two legs). Print I AM SPECIAL across the top of a sheet of white construction paper for each child. Write the memory verse at the bottom.

what to say

God made the earth and everything on it. On the sixth day, God made the first family. First, God made a man and named him Adam. Then God made a woman and named her Eve. When God looked at the man and woman, He liked what He saw and said it was very good. God made the very first family!

What You Need

- ❑ this page, duplicated
- ❑ colored and white construction paper
- ❑ crayons
- ❑ scissors
- ❑ glue sticks

What to Do

1. Allow the students to choose two legs, two arms, a body and a head.
2. Help the children glue the parts onto their papers.
3. Have the students draw the eyes, mouth and nose on the face.
4. As the children work, say, **Each part does something special. Our feet help us to walk. Our eyes help us to see. Our ears help us to hear. We can thank God for making us special.**

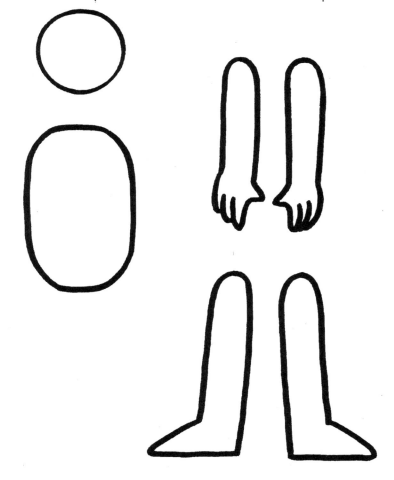

13

Adam and Eve's Family
Beauty All Around Me

Memory Verse

They will be yours for food.
~ Genesis 1:29

Before Class

Cut out trees, flowers, plants, animals and birds from magazines.

what to say

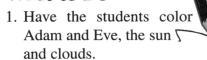

God made a special place for Adam and Eve to live. It was a garden! It had trees with fruit on them and many vegetable plants for them to share with all the animals. Adam and Eve could eat from all the plants and trees but one. The garden was a beautiful place to live. God gave them everything they needed.

What You Need

- ❑ this page, duplicated
- ❑ old magazines
- ❑ crayons
- ❑ scissors
- ❑ glue sticks

What to Do

1. Have the students color Adam and Eve, the sun and clouds.

2. Allow the children to glue trees, flowers, plants, birds and animals on the picture to make a garden.

3. As the students work, say, **Adam and Eve could pick fruit and plants from the garden to eat.** Talk about what kinds of fruit trees and vegetable plants might have been in God's special garden. Say, **Even though people no longer live in special gardens, God still gives us everything we need, too.**

Adam and Eve's Family
Happy Face Reminder

Memory Verse

They hid from the Lord.
~ Genesis 3:8

Before Class

Cut one 6" length of yarn per child.

what to say

In God's garden there were two special trees. God told Adam and Eve they could eat from all of the trees except one. One day, they disobeyed God and ate fruit from the bad tree. They thought they could hide from God, but no one can hide from God. Because they had disobeyed Him, God punished them. Adam and Eve could no longer live in God's beautiful garden.

What You Need

- ❏ this page, duplicated
- ❏ crayons
- ❏ hole punch
- ❏ thin yarn
- ❏ scissors
- ❏ glue sticks

What to Do

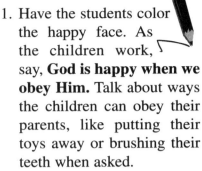

1. Have the students color the happy face. As the children work, say, **God is happy when we obey Him.** Talk about ways the children can obey their parents, like putting their toys away or brushing their teeth when asked.
2. Cut out each child's happy face and punch a hole in the top of it.
3. Give each student a piece of yarn to thread through the hole.
4. Go around and tie the ends of each student's yarn together for hanging at home.

They hid from the Lord.
~ Genesis 3:8

Adam and Eve's Family
Bible Story
Adam and Eve have children.
(Genesis 4:1-2 & Genesis 5:1-2)

First Family Photo

Memory Verse

[God] created them.
~ Genesis 5:2

Before Class

After duplicating page 17, fold each one in half and cut out the rectangle.

what to say

God made the land, water, animals, fish, birds, trees, flowers, fruit and vegetables. He made the sky, sun, moon and stars. God made Adam and Eve and they had two sons. The oldest son was named Cain. The youngest son was named Abel. God's first family was Adam, Eve, Cain and Abel.

What You Need

- page 17, duplicated
- glue sticks
- scissors
- crayons

What to Do

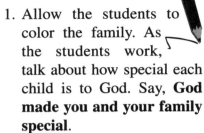

1. Allow the students to color the family. As the students work, talk about how special each child is to God. Say, **God made you and your family special**.
2. Cut out the inner box along the dotted lines. Show how to fold the paper in half so the family shows through.
3. Help the students glue down the sides of the picture frame.

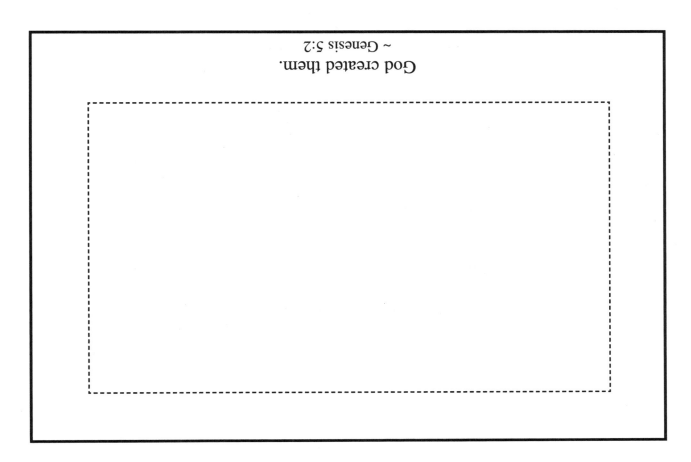

God created them.
~ Genesis 5:2

Fold >

Noah's Family
Praying Children

Memory Verse

Noah...walked with God.
~ Genesis: 6:9

what to say

Noah loved and prayed to God. Noah and his family tried to please God in everything they did. They made God happy. All of the other people did whatever they wanted to do. They didn't love or pray to God. They made God unhappy. It makes God happy when you pray to Him, too.

What You Need

- ❏ this page, duplicated
- ❏ crayons

What to Do

1. Have the students color the picture of the praying children.

2. As the children work, talk about ways to please God, such as obeying parents, taking turns and sharing toys. Explain that God loves to hear our prayers. Say, **There are many ways to please God. We can use our hands to pray to Him. We can sing songs to tell others about our good and loving God. God is happy when we do things to please Him**.

Noah's Family
Animals Everywhere

Memory Verse

Noah did…as God commanded him.
~ Genesis 6:22

Before Class

Cut the chenille wire to fit the ark.

God told Noah there would soon be a flood. He said Noah would need to build a boat called an ark. The ark had to be very big. It had to hold two of every kind of animal! Noah and his family would also live on the ark. Food for everyone had to be stored on the ark. Noah obeyed God. God was pleased with Noah for building the ark.

What You Need

❑ this page, duplicated
❑ crayons
❑ brown chenille wire
❑ glue sticks

What to Do

1. Have the students color the animals and Noah. As the students work, ask them to tell ways that God keeps them safe, such as wearing a seat belt.
2. Help the students glue chenille wires on the ark.
3. Say, **We can please God and do as He asks.**

Noah's Family
Where to Find an Ark

Memory Verse

Go into the ark.
~ Genesis 7:1

Before Class

Bring in pictures of different kinds of boats to share with the children.

 **what to say**

Noah, his wife, their sons and their wives, and all the animals went to live on the ark. Soon it began to rain. It rained for 40 days and 40 nights. Water was everywhere. There was no dry land. God saved Noah, his family, and two of each animal on the ark from the flood. (Show the boat pictures to the children and discuss how large the ark must have been to hold the people and animals.)

What You Need

❑ this page, duplicated
❑ crayons

What to Do

1. Help the students trace the correct path and lead Noah, his family, and the animals to safety on God's ark.
2. As the students work, say, **God watches over each of us all the time.** Talk about how God watches over us, such as while we are asleep, taking a bath or playing.

Noah's Family
The Dove and the Twig

Memory Verse

He…sent out the dove.
~ Genesis 8:10

what to say

Noah, his family and the animals all lived on the ark while it rained for 40 days and nights. The entire earth was under water. After many weeks, the water began to disappear. One day,

Noah sent out a dove to find dry land. When it returned, it had a twig in its beak. Noah knew the land was dry. God showed Noah and his family when it was safe to leave the ark.

What You Need

☐ this page, duplicated
☐ crayons
☐ glue sticks
☐ small twigs

What to Do

1. Have the students color Noah holding the dove. Say, **Doves are white, so you only need to color its beak.**
2. Help the students glue the twig to the dove's beak.

21

Noah's Family
A Promise in the Sky

Memory Verse

I have set my rainbow in the clouds.
~ Genesis 9:13

Before Class

Cut out a rainbow for each child, glue it to poster board and cut it out again. Cut a 6" length of yarn per child.

what to say

Noah and his family lived on an ark until the floodwaters disappeared. When the land was dry, they left the ark. To thank God, Noah built an altar in His honor. God was very happy. He promised Noah that He would never flood the earth again. He gave Noah a sign to remind him. Whenever it rained, God put a rainbow in the sky. God kept His promise to Noah.

What You Need

- [ ] this page, duplicated
- [ ] colored chenille wire
- [ ] hole punch
- [ ] glue sticks
- [ ] poster board
- [ ] scissors
- [ ] yarn

What to Do

1. Help the students glue colored chenille wire on the rainbow to make it colorful. As the students work, ask them if they've ever seen a rainbow.
2. Have the children turn over the rainbow and glue more colored chenille wire to the other side.
3. Punch a hole in each rainbow.
4. Help the students tie a piece of yarn through the hole at the top.
5. Tell the students they can hang the rainbow in their rooms. Say, **When it rains, the rainbow will remind you that God keeps His promises.**

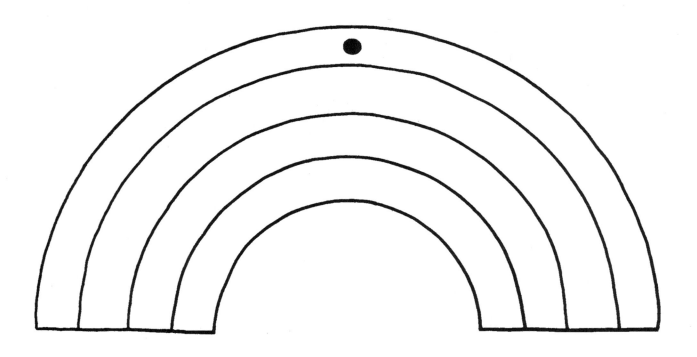

Abraham's Family
Pack Your Bags

Memory Verse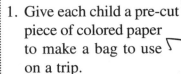

Leave your country.
~ Genesis 12:1

Before Class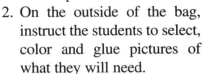

Cut colored paper to about 4 ¼" x 5 ½" for each child. Cut out a set of pictures from below for each child. Cut an 8" length of yarn for each child.

Abram loved and worshipped God. One day, God told him to leave his home, his friends and country. It must have been hard to leave, but Abram obeyed God. He took his wife, his nephew and all their possessions and went to live in Canaan. God was pleased with Abram. He promised to bless Abram and his family.

What You Need

- ❏ this page, duplicated
- ❏ colored paper
- ❏ hole punch
- ❏ scissors
- ❏ yarn

What to Do

1. Give each child a pre-cut piece of colored paper to make a bag to use on a trip.
2. On the outside of the bag, instruct the students to select, color and glue pictures of what they will need.
3. Punch two holes at the top of each bag. Have the students help you thread yarn through the holes for a handle.
4. Write the memory verse on each one.

Abraham's Family
You Go First

Memory Verse

We are brothers.
~ Genesis 13:8

what to say

Abram and his nephew Lot had many sheep, tents and servants. Soon, there were too many sheep and not enough grass for them to eat. The servants who took care of the sheep began to fight. Abram knew the only way to stop the fighting was for one of them to move. Abram gave Lot the choice of where to live. Abram pleased God by letting Lot choose first.

What You Need

- [ ] this page, duplicated
- [ ] crayons
- [ ] glue sticks
- [ ] cotton balls

What to Do

1. Say, **You can please God by letting others be first to choose.** Starting with yourself, let a child choose a crayon first. Then have the children practice letting one another choose the crayon first. Talk about how difficult it can be to let someone else go first, but explain that God likes it when we put other people first.
2. Have the students color the picture of Abram and Lot.
3. Show how to glue cotton balls on the sheep.

Abraham's Family
Glowing Sky

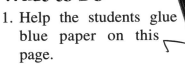

Memory Verse

So shall your offspring be.
~ Genesis 15:5

Before Class

Cut the blue paper into 8½" x 6".

what to say

Abram had a big problem with which only God could help him. Abram had many things that he owned, but he had no children to give them to when he died. When Abram told God about his problem, God told Abram to look up at the night sky. There were so many stars, Abram could not count them. God told him he would have as many family members as there were stars.

What You Need

- ❑ this page, duplicated
- ❑ dark blue construction paper
- ❑ glue sticks
- ❑ flashlight
- ❑ silver star stickers

What to Do

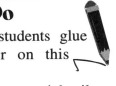

1. Help the students glue blue paper on this page.
2. Allow them to stick silver stars on their blue paper.
3. Turn off the lights and show what happens when you shine a flashlight on the stars. Say, **They glow like the stars in the night sky, don't they? Can you count all of the stars on your paper?**

Abraham's Family
Family Circle

Memory Verse

Your name will be Abraham.
~ Genesis 17:5

 **what to say**

One day, God told Abram that he would be the father of many nations. Then God changed Abram's name to Abraham, which means "father of many." God also changed Abraham's wife's name from Sarai to Sarah, which means "mother of nations." God kept His promise to Abraham. He did become the father of many nations.

What You Need

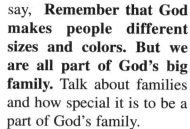

- ❏ page 27, duplicated
- ❏ crayons
- ❏ scissors
- ❏ glue sticks

What to Do

1. Have the students color each person a different color. As they color, say, **Remember that God makes people different sizes and colors. But we are all part of God's big family.** Talk about families and how special it is to be a part of God's family.

2. Cut each student's paper in half.

3. Help the children glue the two pieces together to form a circle. Remind the students that Abraham was the father of many nations.

Your name will be Abraham.

~ Genesis 17:5

CUT ON LINE

Abraham's Family
Promise Keeper

Memory Verse

I have borne him a son.
~ Genesis 21:7

 **what to say**

God promised Abraham and Sarah that they would have a son. At first, Sarah laughed because she was too old to have children. Abraham trusted God and knew He would keep His word. Soon, Sarah became pregnant and gave birth to a son. They named him Isaac. Abraham and Sarah were happy to be parents even though they were old.

What You Need

- ❏ this page, duplicated
- ❏ crayons
- ❏ scissors
- ❏ gold stickers

What to Do

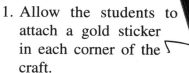

1. Allow the students to attach a gold sticker in each corner of the craft.
2. Instruct the children to color the flowers and letters.
3. Cut out the picture for each student. Explain what a promise is and how important it is to keep it.
4. Say, **You can give this to someone special so he or she will know that God always keeps His promises.**

Isaac's Family
Guess Who?

Memory Verse

There were twin boys.
~ Genesis 25:24

Before Class

Cut the light brown yarn into small pieces and unravel it.

what to say

Isaac was Abraham and Sarah's son. He was 40 years old when he married Rebekah. For 20 years, Isaac and Rebekah had no children. Isaac prayed to God for help. When he was 60 years old, Isaac became the father of twin boys. Esau was born first, then Jacob was born. They were twins but they did not look alike. Esau had hair on his arms and legs. Jacob did not.

What You Need

- ❏ this page, duplicated
- ❏ glue sticks
- ❏ light brown yarn

What to Do

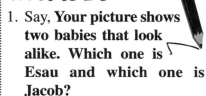

1. Say, **Your picture shows two babies that look alike. Which one is Esau and which one is Jacob?**
2. Give each student some unraveled yarn to glue to Esau's arms and legs.
3. As you help the students, talk about how each baby is a special gift from God.
4. Say, **Now you can tell who is Esau and who is Jacob.**

Isaac's Family
Let's Trade

Memory Verse

Esau despised his birthright.
~ Genesis 25:34

Before Class

Cut out pictures of food from old magazines.

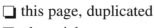 **what to say**

Esau and Jacob were twins. Isaac was their father. Because Esau was born first, he would get a larger portion of everything his father owned. He would also become the family leader when Isaac died. One day, Esau returned home after hunting. He was very hungry. Jacob offered to trade Esau his birthright for food. Without thinking, Esau said yes. Later, Esau was sad that he had traded his birthright to Jacob.

What You Need

☐ this page, duplicated
☐ glue sticks

What to Do

1. Allow the students to glue pictures of food on their "plates" but instruct them to not glue anything in the center of their plates.

2. Say, **Esau sold his birthright for food. That was not a fair trade. Making good choices and being fair pleases God.** Talk about what it means to make good and fair choices, like trading one piece of candy for another rather than three pieces for one piece.

BIRTHRIGHT

Esau despised his birthright.
~ Genesis 25:34

Isaac's Family
Jacob the Pretender

Memory Verse

Your brother...took your blessing.
~ Genesis 27:35

Before Class

Duplicate this page on light brown construction paper and cut out the robe for each child. Unravel some yarn for each child.

what to say

When Isaac was very old and could not see well, he asked Esau to prepare a special meal. Isaac wanted to give Esau, his oldest son, a special blessing. But his mother, Rebekah, wanted Esau's twin, Jacob, to have the blessing instead. She told Jacob to put on Esau's clothes and put goatskins on his hands and neck. Jacob pretended to be Esau so his father would give him the blessing. When Esau found out about this, he was angry.

What You Need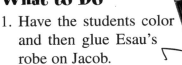

- ❑ pages 31 and 32, duplicated
- ❑ glue sticks
- ❑ light brown construction paper
- ❑ light brown yarn
- ❑ scissors

What to Do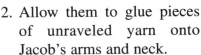

1. Have the students color and then glue Esau's robe on Jacob.
2. Allow them to glue pieces of unraveled yarn onto Jacob's arms and neck.
3. Ask, **Does Jacob now look and feel like Esau? Jacob lied to his father, took the blessing and made his brother very angry. Taking something that does not belong to you is wrong. God wants us to do what is right.**

Your brother...took your blessing.
Genesis 27:35

Isaac's Family
Rock 'N' Oil Altar

Memory Verse

This stone...will be God's house.
~ Genesis 28:22

Before Class

Make rocks by tracing a dime on brown construction paper and cutting five for each child.

what to say

Jacob took Esau's birthright and blessing. This made Esau very mad and he wanted to kill Jacob. Rebekah, their mother, was afraid. She told Jacob to go live with his Uncle Laban. After traveling all day, Jacob laid his head on a rock and fell asleep. In a dream, God told Jacob about all the good things He would do for him. The next morning, Jacob took the rock and poured oil on it to honor God. Now Jacob wanted to serve God.

What You Need

- ❏ this page, duplicated
- ❏ crayons
- ❏ glue sticks
- ❏ brown construction paper

What to Do

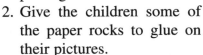

1. Have the students color the picture of Jacob pouring oil on the rock.
2. Give the children some of the paper rocks to glue on their pictures.
3. Ask the children how they feel when they do something wrong. Say, **God forgives us when we do something wrong.**

Will Work for Wife

Memory Verse

Laban had two daughters.
~ Genesis 29:16

Before Class

Cut a green construction paper strip and fringe it with scissors to look like grass. Make one strip per child.

what to say

Jacob traveled a long way until he arrived at the home of Laban, his uncle. Laban invited him to stay with his family. Jacob wanted to marry Rachel, Laban's youngest daughter. Laban made him work for seven years to get to marry Rachel. When it was time to marry her, Laban tricked Jacob into marrying his oldest daughter, Leah, instead. Jacob was mad, so Laban offered to let him marry Rachel also if he worked another seven years. Jacob married Rachel and then worked another seven years for his Uncle Laban.

What You Need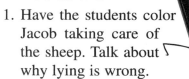

- ❑ this page, duplicated
- ❑ crayons
- ❑ glue sticks
- ❑ green construction paper
- ❑ scissors

What to Do

1. Have the students color Jacob taking care of the sheep. Talk about why lying is wrong.
2. Give each child a grass strip to glue on the picture so the sheep have something to eat.
3. Say, **Laban tricked Jacob just like Jacob had tricked Esau, his brother. God wants us to always tell the truth.**

Isaac's Family
Love Lines

Memory Verse

And they wept.
~ Genesis 33:4

what to say

Jacob lived for many years near his Uncle Laban. One day, God told Jacob to return to his home. Jacob and his family packed their possessions for the long journey. Jacob was still afraid his brother, Esau, wanted to kill him, so he sent servants ahead to tell Esau he was coming home. Esau met Jacob on the road. He hugged and kissed Jacob. Esau had already forgiven him. God had watched over Jacob and brought him back to his brother, Esau.

What You Need

❑ this page, duplicated
❑ crayons
❑ red self-stick hearts

What to Do

1. Have the students connect the lines to make a large heart around Jacob and Esau.
2. Allow them to stick red hearts on Jacob and Esau.
3. Ask the students how they feel when someone hurts them or makes them mad. Say, **We can forgive others when they hurt us or make us mad.** Talk about how good it feels to forgive someone instead of being mad.

Joseph's Family
Torn to Pieces

Memory Verse

He made a...robe for him.
~ Genesis 37:3

Before Class

Tear small pieces of colored paper.

what to say

Joseph had many older brothers. Jacob, his father, gave Joseph a special robe. It was beautiful. It had many colors. Joseph's brothers became jealous of him. One day, they got so mad that they sold him to some people who took him to Egypt. Then they tore his robe and put animal blood on it. When they showed it to their father, Jacob became very sad because he thought Joseph had been killed.

What You Need

- ❑ this page, duplicated
- ❑ colored paper
- ❑ glue sticks

What to Do

1. Help the students glue pieces of colored paper onto Joseph's robe.
2. Talk with the children about how easy it is to get mad and do something wrong, like hit another child. Say, **When people get mad, they sometimes do wrong things. When we get mad, we can stop and ask God to help us do what is right.**

Joseph's Family
I Can Do It

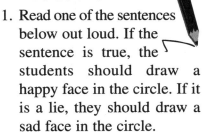

Bible Story
Joseph goes to jail.
(Genesis 39:1-23)

Memory Verse

The Lord was with Joseph.
~ Genesis 39:2

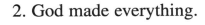

When Joseph was still a boy, he was sold by his brothers to Potiphar, who lived in Egypt. Potiphar was a captain of the guard for Pharaoh, who was the king. One day, Potiphar's wife wanted Joseph to do something bad, but he said no. She was angry, so she told a lie about Joseph. He was arrested and put in jail. Even though bad things happened to Joseph, he still trusted God.

What You Need

- ❏ this page, duplicated
- ❏ crayons

What to Do

1. Read one of the sentences below out loud. If the sentence is true, the students should draw a happy face in the circle. If it is a lie, they should draw a sad face in the circle.

2. Say, **When we tell the truth, God has a happy face. When we lie, He has a sad face. You can tell the truth everyday.** Talk about the consequences of telling a lie versus telling the truth.

1. A dog can drive a car. ◯

2. God made everything. ◯

3. We can learn about Jesus at church. ◯

4. I eat candy for dinner every day. ◯

5. God loves me. ◯

6. I have three legs. ◯

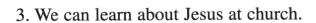
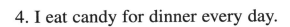

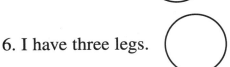

Joseph's Family
A Job for Everyone

Memory Verse

The Lord gave him success.
~ Genesis 39:3

what to say

While Joseph was in jail, he trusted God and did what He wanted him to do. There were many people in jail. One man had been the baker for the Pharaoh, the king of Egypt. Another man tasted the food and drink for Pharaoh. He was called a cupbearer. Joseph helped the two men. They promised to tell the king when they got out of jail. But they forgot, and Joseph stayed in jail.

What You Need

☐ this page, duplicated
☐ crayons
☐ food stickers

What to Do

1. Give the students stickers to put on their plates.
2. Instruct them to color the drinks in the glasses, as well as the rest of the page.

3. Say, **Joseph worked for God even while he was in jail. His job was to do good, help others and trust in God. You can trust God no matter where you are. God has a special job just for you!** Talk about how the children can work for God by helping and obeying their parents. Explain how God takes care of them no matter where they are.

Joseph's Family
A Walking Billboard

Memory Verse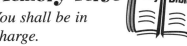

You shall be in charge.
~ Genesis 41:40

Before Class

Cut four 9" pieces of yarn per child.

what to say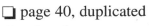

While Joseph was in jail, Pharaoh, the king of Egypt, had two dreams. Pharaoh heard Joseph could tell what dreams meant, so he sent for him. Joseph told him what the dreams meant. Pharaoh was very pleased with Joseph and let him out of jail. Then Joseph became the Pharaoh's special helper. Everyone had to obey Joseph. God watched over Joseph. He had a special plan for his life.

What You Need

- ❏ page 40, duplicated
- ❏ colored paper
- ❏ crayons
- ❏ string
- ❏ hole punch

What to Do

1. Have the students color the letters on the front of their billboard on page 40.
2. When they are finished, punch a hole in each side and at the top right and left of the billboard.
3. Put string through each hole and tie a knot in each end.
4. Hold the sign on the child while you tie the strings behind his or her neck and back, like an apron.
5. Say, **Now you can show everyone that God watches over you.** Talk about how God never sleeps or takes a vacation, but watches over us day and night.

39

GOD

WATCHES

OVER

ME

Joseph's Family
Filled to the Brim

Memory Verse

Seven years of famine began.
~ Genesis 41:54

what to say

Joseph was now 30 years old. He trusted, loved and worshipped God while he was a slave. God had warned Joseph that there would be a famine soon, which means there would be no food. Joseph told Pharaoh, the king of Egypt, about the famine. The king knew Joseph was a wise man, so he put him in charge of everyone. Joseph told the people to save some of their crops each year so that when the famine came, they would have food to eat. Joseph was no longer a slave.

What You Need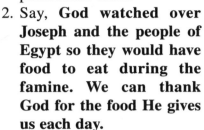

- ❏ this page, duplicated
- ❏ crayons
- ❏ glue
- ❏ dry pasta shapes

What to Do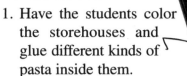

1. Have the students color the storehouses and glue different kinds of pasta inside them.

2. Say, **God watched over Joseph and the people of Egypt so they would have food to eat during the famine. We can thank God for the food He gives us each day.**

3. Encourage the students to remember to say a prayer before they eat, thanking God for taking care of them.

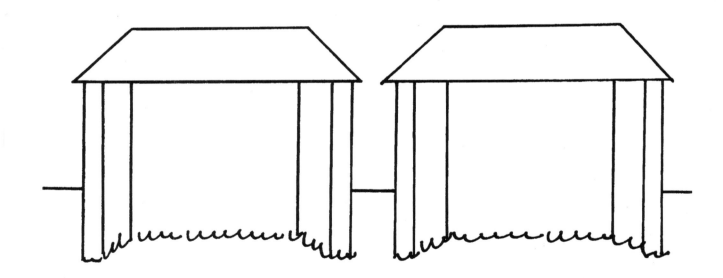

Joseph's Family
A Peace Offering

Memory Verse

I am Joseph!
~ Genesis 45:3

Before Class

Cut out the rectangle on the lesson page.

 what to say

There was a famine not only in Egypt, but also in Canaan where Joseph's family lived. Joseph had been away for almost 13 years and lived in Egypt as a slave. Pharaoh, the king of Egypt, saw how wise Joseph was and put him in charge of everyone. Joseph was now a free man. When Joseph's brothers came to Egypt to buy grain, they didn't know who he was. Joseph recognized his brothers and forgave them.

What You Need

- ❏ this page, duplicated
- ❏ happy face stickers
- ❏ scissors

What to Do

1. Help the students attach happy face stickers to each corner of their Peace Offering.
2. Say, **Joseph forgave his brothers even though they were mean to him. Joseph knew that God wanted him to make peace with them. You can forgive others when they are mean to you, too**.

I FORGIVE YOU

Moses' Family
Safe with a New Mom

Memory Verse

She named him Moses.
~ Exodus 2:10

Before Class

Cut out two rectangles and one baby for each child. Cut six ½" x 5" strips and eight ½" x 2½" strips from brown construction paper for each child.

When God's people lived in Egypt, the new king was bad and didn't like them. Baby Moses' mother was afraid, so she made a basket and put him in it. Then she placed the basket in the grass growing in the Nile River. She hoped someone would find her baby and keep him safe. A nice woman found Moses and took him home. God watched over Moses and kept him safe.

What You Need

- ❏ page 44, duplicated
- ❏ brown construction paper
- ❏ glue sticks
- ❏ scissors

What to Do

1. Help the students glue three strips of brown paper going top to bottom on the front and back of the basket (the two rectangles).
2. Help them glue four strips of brown paper going side to side on the front and back of the basket.
3. Assist the students in gluing the two sides and bottom of the basket together, then set baby Moses inside the basket. Say, **God kept baby Moses safe and He can keep you safe.**

Finished Craft

Moses Runs Away

Memory Verse

Moses was afraid.
~ Exodus 2:14

 what to say

The bad king of Egypt made all of God's people become slaves. Moses was one of God's people, but he was raised by the Egyptian princess, so he was not a slave. One day, Moses saw an Egyptian man hitting one of the slaves. This made him so mad that he killed the man. When the bad king found out, he wanted to hurt Moses. Moses was afraid and ran away to the desert to live.

What You Need

❏ this page, duplicated
❏ crayons

What to Do

1. Have the students color the picture of Moses running away.

2. Say, **Moses did a bad thing when he killed the Egyptian man, even though the man was hurting one of God's people. Instead of hitting someone who has hit you first, you can tell the person that it isn't nice to hit.** Talk about what the children can do when they want to hit or push someone who has been mean to them.

Moses' Family
God's Voice in the Desert

Memory Verse

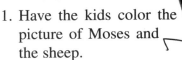

Moses said, "Here I am."
~ Exodus 3:4

Before Class

For each child, cut several red and yellow paper strips with pointed tops that look like flames.

 **what to say**

Moses ran away after he killed a man. He lived near the desert and stayed with a family who raised sheep. He married one of the daughters and began a new life. One day while Moses was watching over the sheep, he saw a burning bush. He walked closer. Suddenly, God called out to Moses. Moses answered God by saying, "Here I am." God told Moses that He was going to free His people from the Egyptians.

What You Need

- ❑ this page, duplicated
- ❑ glue sticks
- ❑ crayons
- ❑ yellow and red paper

What to Do

1. Have the kids color the picture of Moses and the sheep.
2. Help the students glue red and yellow pieces of paper onto the bush.
3. Say, **When you pray, you are talking to God. You can pray anytime or anywhere! He always hears your prayers.** Talk about how God loves to hear our prayers.

Moses' Family
The Truthful Staff

Bible Story
God calls Moses to serve Him.
(Exodus 3:1-4:20)

Memory Verse

I will help you speak.
~ Exodus 4:12

Before Class

Cut two 2" lengths of brown chenille wire for each child. Form one into a simple staff. Curl the other one around a pencil to form a snake.

 **what to say**

God told Moses to go to Egypt and bring His people to a new land. Moses complained to God because he didn't think he could talk well enough for the people to listen to him. God gave Moses a staff that he could turn into a snake to prove that he was saying what God wanted him to say. Aaron, Moses' brother, went with him to Egypt. God promised to teach them both what to say.

What You Need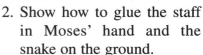

- ❏ this page, duplicated
- ❏ crayons
- ❏ glue
- ❏ brown chenille wire

What to Do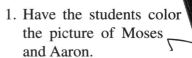

1. Have the students color the picture of Moses and Aaron.
2. Show how to glue the staff in Moses' hand and the snake on the ground.
3. Say, **God's words are in the Bible. The Bible is always true.** Talk about words that are true.

Moses' Family
Freedom Roll

Memory Verse

Let my people go.
~ Exodus 8:1

Before Class

Cut the toilet paper rolls in half, one half per child. Cut out the plague strips for each child.

 **what to say**

God told Moses to go to Pharaoh and tell him to let God's people go. When Moses complained to God that he didn't know how to talk well enough, God said that Aaron, Moses' brother, would speak for him. Moses and Aaron did as God asked. They went to Pharaoh and told him to let God's people go. Pharaoh said, "No." Then God sent a plague. Moses and Aaron asked Pharaoh many times, but he always said, "No." God sent many more plagues.

What You Need

- ❏ this page, duplicated
- ❏ crayons
- ❏ glue sticks
- ❏ tape
- ❏ toilet paper rolls

What to Do

1. Help the students tape the three strips together into one long strip.
2. Show how to tape the top of the first plague to a pre-cut cardboard roll.
3. Help the children roll the plagues around the cardboard.
4. Say, **You can show others the plagues God sent when Pharaoh said, "No." How would you feel if there were frogs or flies everywhere?**

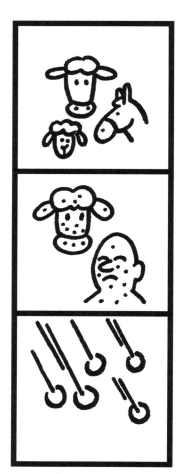

Moses' Family
Dry to Cross

Memory Verse

Do not be afraid.
~ Exodus 14:13

Before Class
Cut out a set of Red Sea pieces for each child. Cut the slits where shown on a copy of page 50 for each child.

what to say

When Pharaoh let God's people go, Moses and Aaron led them into the desert. When they reached the Red Sea and looked back, they saw Pharaoh's army chasing them. Pharaoh had changed his mind! God parted the Red Sea so His people could cross to the other side without getting wet. When Pharaoh's army tried to cross, God made the sea full of water again. All of God's people were safe, but none of Pharaoh's army made it to the dry land.

What You Need

- ❏ pages 49 and 50, duplicated
- ❏ crayons
- ❏ scissors

What to Do

1. Allow the students to color the picture of God's people walking across the dry Red Sea, and the Red Sea inserts.
2. Help the children put the Red Sea into the slots so that it covers the people.
3. Show how to pull the Red Sea tabs apart to reveal God's people crossing the sea.
4. Say, **God's people crossed without getting wet. God helps us every day and keeps us safe.**

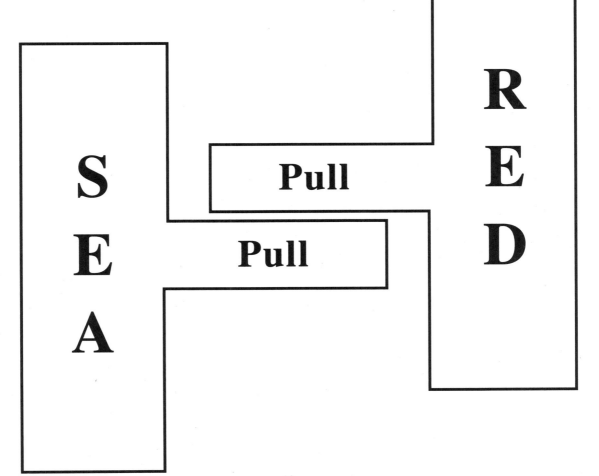

Do not be afraid.
~ Exodus 14:13

Moses' Family
Broken Pieces

Memory Verse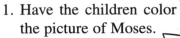

I will write on them.
~ Exodus 34:1

Before Class

Trace the broken tablets on gray construction paper and cut two for each child.

what to say

God called Moses and Aaron to come up Mount Sinai so He could tell them the rules for the people to obey. After awhile, Aaron went back down the mountain but Moses stayed so God could write the rules on two stone tablets. Moses was gone a long time. Everyone thought he had died. They began to do bad things. When Moses came down and saw the people, he got angry and broke the stone tablets. Then God made new tablets.

What You Need

- ☐ this page, duplicated
- ☐ glue sticks
- ☐ construction paper
- ☐ crayons
- ☐ scissors

What to Do

1. Have the children color the picture of Moses.
2. Give the students two new stone tablets to glue on top of the broken ones.
3. Say, **God is happy when we obey Him. When we get mad, like Moses, God is unhappy.**

Moses' Family
Hitting Isn't Nice

Memory Verse

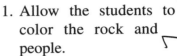

Speak to that rock.
~ Numbers 20:8

Before Class

Cut a few thin strips of blue construction paper for each child.

what to say

Moses, Aaron and God's people wandered in the desert for a long time. Some people complained because there was no water. God told Moses to speak to the rock and it would give them water. The people became demanding, so Moses got angry and struck the rock with his staff. Then God became angry with him because Moses had hit the rock instead of speaking to it. Moses disobeyed God.

What You Need

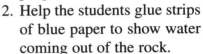

- ❏ this page, duplicated
- ❏ glue
- ❏ crayons
- ❏ blue construction paper
- ❏ scissors

What to Do

1. Allow the students to color the rock and people.
2. Help the students glue strips of blue paper to show water coming out of the rock.
3. Say, **You can make God happy by obeying your parents when they ask you to help clean up your toys.** Talk about ways the kids can make God happy: obeying their parents, sharing and being kind to other children.

Ruth's Family
A Sad Good-bye

Memory Verse

Where you go I will go.
~ Ruth 1:16

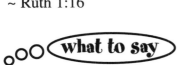

what to say

A man named Elimelech took his wife, Naomi, and their two sons to live in another country. His sons married women there. When Elimelech and both sons died, Naomi decided to return to her old country to live. She told her daughters-in-law to stay with their families and find new husbands. Ruth, one of the daughters-in-law, loved Naomi and didn't want to leave her. So Ruth went with Naomi back to her country.

What You Need

❑ this page, duplicated
❑ crayons

What to Do

1. Have the students connect the dots in the picture of Ruth saying good-bye to her family and friends.

2. Say, **It must have been difficult for Ruth to leave her family and go with Naomi to a new country. Ruth showed kindness and love to Naomi. You can be kind to others who are new in your class.** Talk about how exciting and scary it was for Ruth to travel to a new country. Ask the students if they have ever gone on a trip to a new place and how they felt.

Ruth's Family
Love Gleans a Field

Memory Verse

*May the Lord
repay you.*
~ Ruth 2:12

what to say

Ruth and Naomi traveled to Bethlehem. Both of their husbands had died. Ruth loved Naomi, her mother-in-law, and wanted to take care of her. She found a field that was being harvested and collected the grain the workers had missed. Boaz, the man who owned the field, saw Ruth. He had heard how she showed love and kindness to Naomi, his relative. He let Ruth continue to work in his field so she and Naomi would have food to eat.

What You Need

- ☐ this page, duplicated
- ☐ crayons
- ☐ glue sticks
- ☐ pasta shapes

What to Do

1. Have the students color the picture of Ruth.
2. Show how to glue pasta shapes in the baskets.
3. Say, **When Ruth finished in the field, her basket was full! Ruth showed Naomi love and kindness by picking grain so they would have food to eat.** Talk about ways the students can show kindness to others by sharing their crayons, toys and books. Ask the students to count the pasta shapes in their baskets.

Ruth's Family
Pin a Ribbon on Me

Memory Verse

She...became his wife.
~ Ruth 4:13

what to say

Naomi was very wise. She knew God wanted Ruth to get married and have children. She also knew it would be good if Ruth married Boaz. Naomi told Ruth how to let Boaz know she was ready for marriage. Boaz loved Ruth and knew God would be pleased if he married her. Boaz also took care of Naomi, who was his relative. After Boaz and Ruth got married, they had a son. Naomi was very happy.

What You Need

- ❏ this page, duplicated
- ❏ crayons
- ❏ scissors
- ❏ medium-size safety pins

What to Do

1. Allow the students to color the ribbon.
2. Before the children leave, cut out their ribbons and pin them on them.
3. Say, **When people see the ribbon, they will know that you want to please God.** Give the students examples of how they can please God: by picking up their toys, sharing with others, and taking their turn.

Hannah's Family
Hands That Pray

Memory Verse

I asked the Lord for him.
~ 1 Samuel 1:20

Before Class

Write the words I CAN PRAY at the bottom of a plate and cut a 6" length of yarn for each child.

 **what to say**

Hannah was married to Elkanah for many years, but they had no children. Hannah loved and worshipped God. One day, she went to the temple to pray to God for a child. While she was there, she met Eli, the priest. He saw her praying. The priest told her to go in peace because God would give her a child. Soon, Hannah gave birth to a son. God answered Hannah's prayer.

What You Need

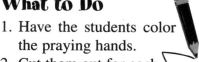

- ❏ this page, duplicated
- ❏ 9" paper plates
- ❏ scissors
- ❏ yarn
- ❏ glue
- ❏ crayons
- ❏ hole punch

What to Do

1. Have the students color the praying hands.
2. Cut them out for each child.
3. Allow the students to glue the hands to the center of a paper plate.
4. Punch two holes at the top of each child's plate. Thread and tie the yarn through the holes so the plate will hang.
5. Say, **You can pray to God each night.**

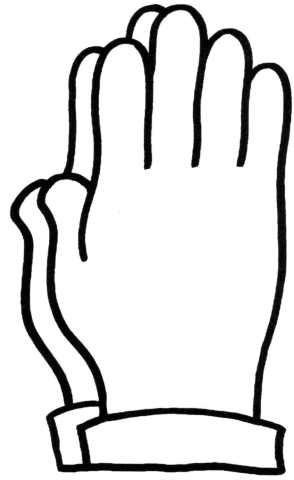

Hannah's Family
A Mother's Gift of Love

Memory Verse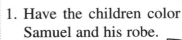

*I give him to
the Lord.*
~ 1 Samuel 1:28

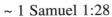 **what to say**

God answered Hannah's prayer to have a child. After she gave birth to her son, she named him Samuel. The name Samuel means "asked of God." Hannah promised God she would give her child to Him. When Samuel was 3 years old, Hannah took him to Eli, the priest. She told him of her promise. Eli raised the boy to know, love and worship God. Each year, Hannah went to visit Samuel and to give him a special robe she made.

What You Need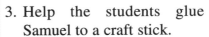

- [ ] this page, duplicated
- [ ] glue sticks
- [ ] 6" craft sticks
- [ ] scissors
- [ ] crayons

What to Do

1. Have the children color Samuel and his robe.
2. Cut out Samuel and his robe for each child.
3. Help the students glue Samuel to a craft stick.
4. Show how to fit the robe on Samuel. Put a dab of glue on the tabs of the robe to help it stay on.
5. Say, **Hannah loved her son, Samuel, and wanted the best for him.** Talk about good things the students' parents do for them.

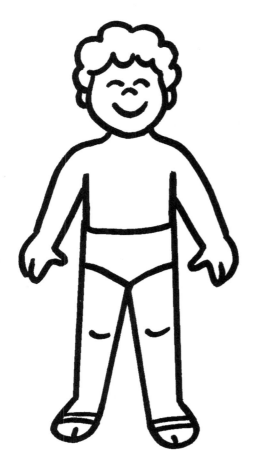

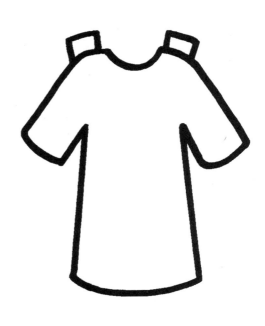

Hannah's Family
My Joy Book

Memory Verse

My heart rejoices.
~ 1 Samuel 2:1

Before Class

Fold two sheets of paper together to make a book for each child. Punch two holes on the folded side. Cut a 6" length of yarn for each child. Cut out pictures of things for which they can thank God (food, clothes, parents, etc.).

Hannah was married for many years but she had no children. She prayed to God to give her a child and God answered her. After Samuel was born, Hannah praised God and told Him she had found joy in the Lord. When Hannah praised God to thank Him, He was pleased and blessed her. It is good to thank God for who He is and what He does.

What You Need

- ❏ this page, duplicated
- ❏ 8½" x 11" white paper
- ❏ glue sticks
- ❏ yarn
- ❏ hole punch
- ❏ scissors
- ❏ marker

What to Do

1. Encourage the children to select pictures of things for which they can thank God and glue them in their Joy Book.
2. Write "My Joy Book" on the cover, then tie the book together.
3. Say, **God likes to hear us thank Him for all the good things He gives us.**

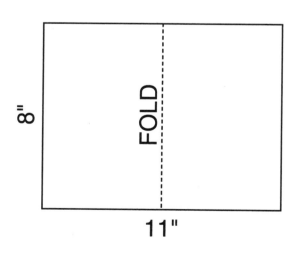

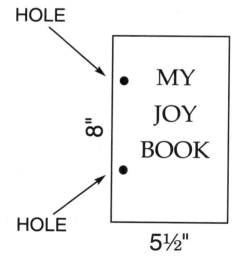

Hannah's Family
From Promises to Blessings

Memory Verse

The Lord was gracious to Hannah.
~ 1 Samuel 2:21

what to say

Hannah made a promise to God even before her son was born. When Samuel was 3 years old, she took him to the temple to live with Eli, the priest. He raised Samuel to serve God when he got older. Because Hannah kept her promise, God blessed her with five more children: three boys and two girls. Hannah's family grew from no children to six, all because she loved God.

What You Need

- ❑ page 60, duplicated
- ❑ watercolor paints
- ❑ paintbrushes
- ❑ paint smocks
- ❑ paper towels

What to Do

1. Dress the students in paint smocks (men's old shirts) to protect their clothing.
2. Allow the children to paint the picture of Hannah's family.
3. Say, **Hannah kept her promise to God. He blessed her with five more children. We need to keep our promises to God and He will bless us.** Explain to the children that a promise is telling someone you will do something, and then doing it.

Hannah's Family

The Lord was gracious to Hannah.
1 Samuel 2:21

Calling All Prophets

Memory Verse

The Lord called Samuel.
~ 1 Samuel 3:4

Before Class

Cut a 3" length of yarn for each child.

what to say

When Samuel was still young, God called him to be a prophet. A prophet is a person who speaks for God. When God wanted His people to know something very important, He told Samuel first. Then Samuel told the people what God had told him about how they were supposed to live. God wanted them to worship only Him.

What You Need

- this page, duplicated
- crayons
- glue
- yarn

What to Do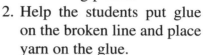

1. Allow the children to color the picture of the two kids talking on a string phone.
2. Help the students put glue on the broken line and place yarn on the glue.
3. Say, **You can tell your friends what you learn about God in Sunday school each week.** Talk about all the wonderful things they can tell others about God, like how much He loves them.

David's Family
Size Doesn't Matter

Memory Verse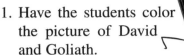

Your servant will...fight him.
~ 1 Samuel 17:32

what to say

David had seven brothers. Some of them fought against the Philistines. The Philistines had a giant named Goliath. He was over nine feet tall! David's father sent him to find his brothers to see if they were well. When David heard the men talking about Goliath, he offered to fight him. David was a small boy. He had only a slingshot and some stones to fight Goliath, but God helped David. He hit Goliath in his forehead with a stone and Goliath died.

What You Need

- [ ] this page, duplicated
- [ ] round brown stickers
- [ ] crayons

What to Do

1. Have the students color the picture of David and Goliath.
2. Allow them to put stickers on the pile of stones.
3. Ask, **How many stones did David have?** Help the children count the stones.
4. Say, **God used David even though he was smaller than Goliath. God protects everyone, no matter how small they are. God protects you.** Ask the students how God takes care of them.

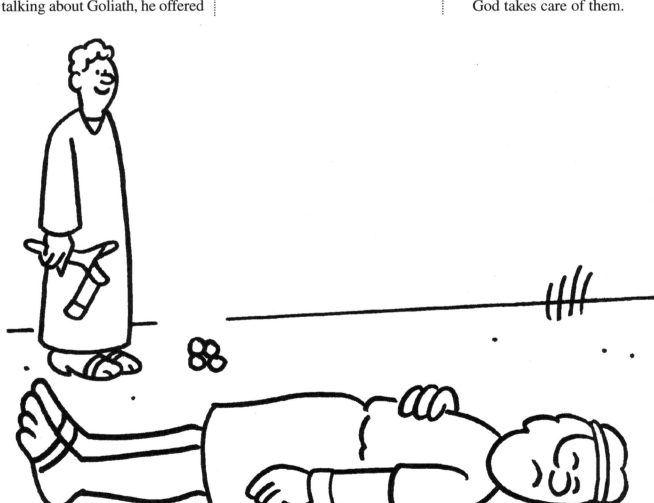

David's Family
A King Who Worships God

Memory Verse

They anointed David king.
~ 2 Samuel 2:4

 **what to say**

The people of Israel wanted a king. God told Samuel, the prophet, to have a man named Saul become king. At first, King Saul worshipped and obeyed God. Then he began to do only what he wanted. God became angry with King Saul and said he could not be king anymore.

When King Saul died, David became the new king. King David loved, worshipped and obeyed God.

What You Need

- ❏ this page, duplicated
- ❏ crayons
- ❏ glue sticks
- ❏ large, flat sequins

What to Do

1. Allow the students to color the picture of King Saul and King David.
2. Show how to glue "jewels" to their crown.
3. Have the students circle the king that loved, worshipped and obeyed God.
4. Say, **You can show God you love Him by singing songs and learning your memory verses.** Explain how they can worship God by praying, singing and listening during story time.

King David worships God   King Saul admires himself

63

David's Family
Like Father, Like Son

Memory Verse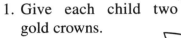

Solomon…shall be king.
~ 1 Kings 1:30

Before Class

Make patterns from the crowns in the picture below and trace them on gold construction paper. Cut two for each child.

 what to say

King David married a woman named Bathsheba. They had a baby boy and named him Solomon. King David wanted a son who would grow up and become the next king. He also knew that God would want the next king of Israel to love and worship only Him. King David had other sons, but he promised Bathsheba that Solomon would be the next king. God was pleased with David.

What You Need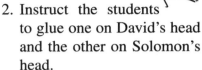

- ☐ this page, duplicated
- ☐ gold construction paper
- ☐ glue sticks
- ☐ crayons
- ☐ scissors

What to Do

1. Give each child two gold crowns.
2. Instruct the students to glue one on David's head and the other on Solomon's head.
3. Allow the students to color the rest of the picture.
4. Say, **King David taught his son, Solomon, about God. Your parents bring you to church so you can learn about God, too.**

King David

King David & Bathsheba

Baby Solomon

King Solomon

David's Family
A Temple for God

Memory Verse
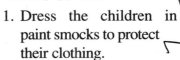

*Solomon built
the temple.*
~ 1 Kings 6:14

Before Class

Cut the sponges into 1" x 1" squares.

what to say

King David taught Solomon to obey God. When Solomon became king of Israel, God appeared to him in a dream. He asked King Solomon what he wanted from Him. Solomon answered that he wanted to be wise. Then King Solomon decided to build a special building in which to worship God. This building was called a temple. It took many years to build. It was beautiful.

What You Need

- ☐ this page, duplicated
- ☐ gold, water-based paint
- ☐ paint smocks
- ☐ sponges
- ☐ paper towels

What to Do

1. Dress the children in paint smocks to protect their clothing.
2. Show how to dip a sponge in gold paint and press it on the walls of the temple.
3. Say, **King Solomon built the temple for God. People came to the temple to worship God. You can worship Him at church, in Sunday school or anywhere!**

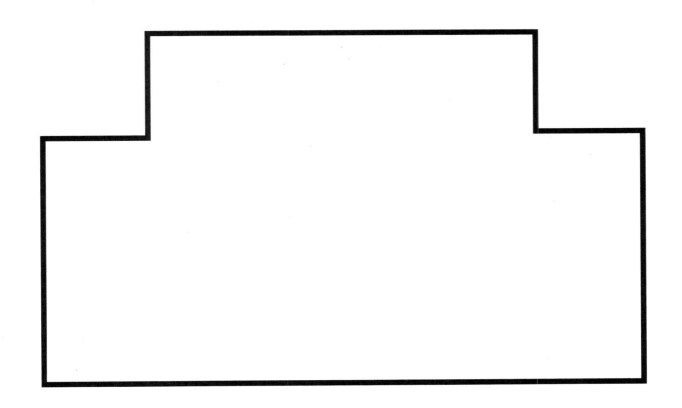

Esther's Family
To Be or Not to Be Queen

Memory Verse

He…made her queen.
~ Esther 2:17

Before Class

Trace the crown and strap and cut one set for each child.

what to say

Esther lived with her cousin Mordecai. When she was young, her parents died. Mordecai took care of her. Both Esther and Mordecai were Jews and worshipped God. King Xerxes ruled the country. He was looking for a new queen. Esther and many other young women were taken to him. Mordecai told Esther not to tell anyone she was Jewish. King Xerxes saw how beautiful Esther was and chose her to be his queen. God had a plan for Esther.

What You Need

- ❏ page 67, duplicated
- ❏ gold paper
- ❏ large, flat sequins
- ❏ glue
- ❏ stapler
- ❏ tape

What to Do

1. Give each child a crown and allow them to glue the "jewels" (sequins) on it.
2. After they are finished, staple a strap to each child's crown and adjust it for fit, cutting off any extra. Place tape over the staples to prevent injury.
3. As the children wear their crowns, say, **It's fun to pretend to be a king or queen, but Esther was a real queen. She wore a beautiful crown.** Ask how it would feel to be queen and what queens do. Say, **Esther was a queen who loved God. He made her queen so she could work for Him.**

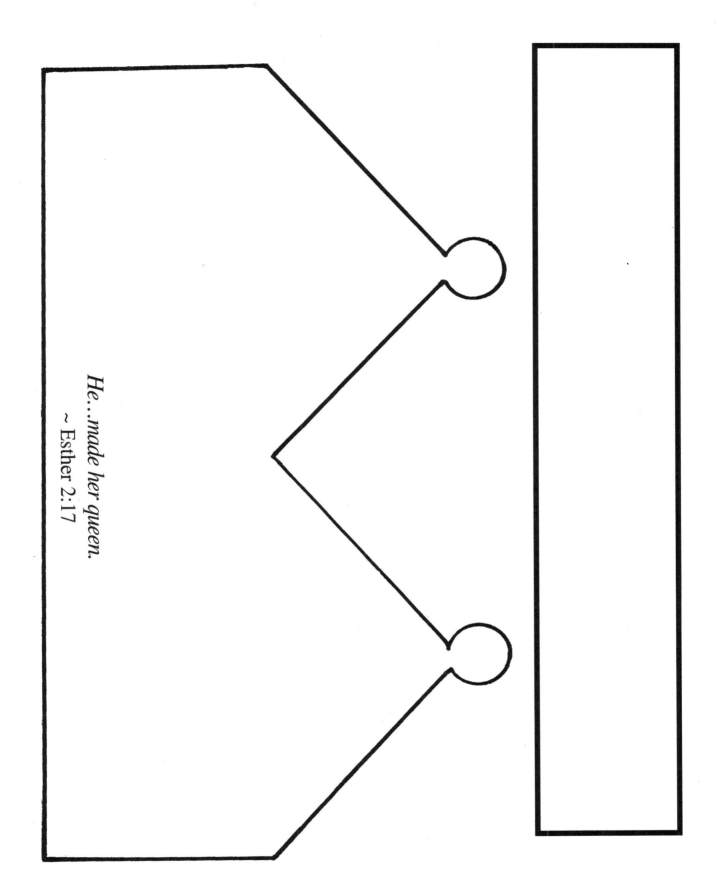

He...made her queen.
~ Esther 2:17

Esther's Family
Good News Megaphone

Bible Story
Esther and Mordecai save
the king. (Esther 2:19-23)

Memory Verse

*Mordecai...told
Queen Esther.*
~ Esther 2:22

Before Class

Bring in pictures, cut from magazines or newspapers, that the children can use to tell others about Jesus: phone, microphone, newspaper, TV and radio.

 **what to say**

Esther was a young, Jewish woman who was raised by her cousin Mordecai. King Xerxes chose her to be his queen. One day while Mordecai was sitting at the king's gate, he heard two of the king's officers talking about killing the king. Mordecai told Queen Esther, who told King Xerxes. Mordecai and Queen Esther saved King Xerxes' life.

What You Need

❏ this page, duplicated
❏ crayons
❏ stapler
❏ tape

What to Do

1. Give two megaphones to each child. Allow the students to color the megaphones.
2. Cut the megaphones out, place them together back-to-back, and tape them at the top and bottom.
3. Say, **Queen Esther told the truth to the king and it saved his life. You can use your megaphone to tell others the truth that Jesus loves them.** Show the students your Bible and explain that the Bible is the best place to find the truth for life.

Esther's Family
Worship Only God

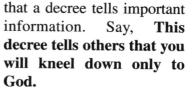

Memory Verse

*Mordecai would not
kneel down.*
~ Esther 3:2

 what to say

Haman was one of King Xerxes' top officials. People were supposed to kneel down to him. Mordecai would not kneel down to anyone except God. Haman told King Xerxes that some people were not obeying this rule. King Xerxes told Haman he could punish the disobedient people. Haman plotted to have the Jews killed. Haman didn't know that Queen Esther was a Jew.

What You Need

❏ this page, duplicated
❏ crayons

What to Do

1. Allow the students to color the decree. Explain that a decree tells important information. Say, **This decree tells others that you will kneel down only to God.**

2. Explain that we can kneel when we pray to God, such as next to our beds at night. Talk about why we should honor God (because He is our creator, He loves us and takes care of us). Explain that He is the only God.

DECREE

I WILL KNEEL DOWN ONLY TO GOD

Esther's Family
Food for a King

Memory Verse

I will go to the king.
~ Esther 4:16

what to say

Haman was a bad man who worked for the king. He planned to kill all of the Jews in the country, but he didn't know Queen Esther was a Jew. Mordecai asked his cousin Queen Esther to help. She invited King Xerxes and Haman to a dinner. The king loved Queen Esther and told her she could have anything she wanted. She asked him to save her life and the lives of her people. He promised he would do as she asked.

What You Need

- ❑ this page, duplicated
- ❑ crayons

What to Do

1. Have the students color the pictures of food.
2. Instruct them to circle the food they like to eat.
3. Say, **At Christmas, Thanksgiving and on birthdays, families eat special food and decorate their tables. King Xerxes and Haman felt special when Queen Esther invited them to dinner.** Talk about the special foods the children eat at Christmas or a birthday party.

Esther's Family
Saved

Memory Verse

What honor...has Mordecai received?
~ Esther 6:3

Before Class

Trace Mordecai's robe below and cut one from purple paper for each child.

Mordecai and Queen Esther were cousins, but they were also Jews. When the king found out Haman ordered all the Jews to be killed, he ordered Haman to be killed. Because Mordecai helped save the king's life, the king wanted to honor Mordecai. King Xerxes gave him a royal robe to wear. Then the king gave Haman's job to Mordecai. God used Mordecai, Queen Esther and even King Xerxes to save the lives of the Jews.

What You Need

- ❏ this page, duplicated
- ❏ purple paper
- ❏ scissors
- ❏ glue sticks

What to Do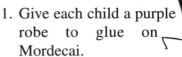

1. Give each child a purple robe to glue on Mordecai.
2. Say, **God used Queen Esther and Mordecai to save King Xerxes. God then used King Xerxes to save Queen Esther, Mordecai and all the Jewish people.** Explain to the children how God can use them to do good things, such as helping their parents.

Jesus' Family
A Special Message

Memory Verse

I am the Lord's servant.
~ Luke 1:38

what to say

Mary and Joseph were engaged to be married. One day, God sent an angel to tell Mary something special. The angel Gabriel told Mary she would become the mother of the Son of God. She was to name her baby Jesus. Mary was both happy and afraid. The angel also told her God would take care of her. Mary trusted God.

What You Need

- ❏ this page, duplicated
- ❏ crayons
- ❏ glue sticks
- ❏ thin pretzel sticks

What to Do

1. Have the students color the picture of Gabriel talking to Mary. While they color, talk about how God takes care of them by providing food, a bed to sleep on, clothes and loving parents.
2. Help the children put glue on the lines around Gabriel.
3. Help them place pretzel sticks on the glue. Be sure to bring extra pretzel sticks for snacking.
4. Say, **Mary trusted God and knew He would take care of her. You can trust God to take care of you, too.**

Jesus' Family
Happy Mother-to-Be

Memory Verse

My soul glorifies the Lord.
~ Luke 1:46

what to say

The angel Gabriel told Mary that she would be Jesus' mother. Gabriel also told her that Elizabeth, her relative, would have a baby. But Elizabeth was too old to have children! When Mary went to visit Elizabeth, she knew the angel had been right. Elizabeth was going to have a baby! Then Mary remembered that the angel told her that with God nothing is impossible. Mary was very happy and began to praise God.

What You Need

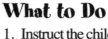

❏ this page, duplicated
❏ crayons

What to Do

1. Instruct the children to color Mary and Elizabeth.
2. Have them draw a happy face on each one.
3. Ask the students what makes them happy. Say, **God loves us and wants us to be happy. Your can be happy because you come to Sunday school and learn about Jesus.**

Jesus' Family
Angel in My Dream

Memory Verse

*An angel...
appeared to him.*
~ Matthew 1:20

Before Class

Cut a piece of poster board to fit the angel for each child.

what to say

Mary told Joseph she was going to have a special baby. She said He would be the Son of God. At first, Joseph was angry, so he decided not to marry her. Then one of God's angels appeared to Joseph in a dream and told him that Mary's baby would be Jesus, the Savior. God wanted Joseph to make Mary his wife. Joseph obeyed God's Word.

What You Need

- ❏ this page, duplicated
- ❏ scissors
- ❏ crayons
- ❏ glue sticks
- ❏ poster board
- ❏ self-stick magnet strips

What to Do

1. Have the students color the angel.
2. Cut out the angel for each child.
3. Help the students glue their angels onto pieces of poster board.
4. Help the students stick a magnet on the back.
5. Say, **Now you can put your angel on your refrigerator at home. God used an angel to help Joseph understand His plan for him. God loves us and sends His angels to watch over us.** Ask the children what they think angels do each day.

An angel... appeared to him.
Matthew 1:20

Jesus' Family
Straw for the Manger

Memory Verse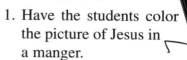

A Savior has been born.
~ Luke 2:11

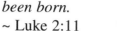

what to say

Joseph and Mary traveled to Bethlehem. There were so many people that there was no place for them to stay. They had to sleep in a stable. While they were there, Mary gave birth to baby Jesus. In a nearby field, there were shepherds taking care of their sheep. Angels appeared and told them a Savior had been born. Then the shepherds went to find Him. When they saw baby Jesus, the shepherds praised God.

What You Need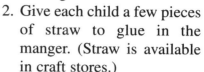

- ❑ this page, duplicated
- ❑ crayons
- ❑ glue sticks
- ❑ straw

What to Do

1. Have the students color the picture of Jesus in a manger.
2. Give each child a few pieces of straw to glue in the manger. (Straw is available in craft stores.)
3. Say, **God gave us Jesus to be our Savior. He can be your Savior, too.** Talk about how we celebrate the birth of Jesus at Christmas because He is our Savior.

Jesus' Family
Visitors from Afar

Memory Verse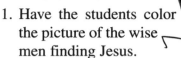

They...worshipped him.
~ Matthew 2:11

Before Class

Shape the chenille wire to fit the outside shape of the star, one per child.

what to say

When Jesus was born, there was a special star in the sky. One night, some wise men saw this special star. They followed it until it stopped over the place where Joseph, Mary and Jesus lived. It took a long time to get there! The wise men bowed down and worshipped Jesus. Then they gave Him gifts. They were happy that God had given them the special star to follow so they could see the Savior.

What You Need

- ❏ page 77, duplicated
- ❏ glue
- ❏ crayons
- ❏ gold chenille wire

What to Do

1. Have the students color the picture of the wise men finding Jesus.
2. Give each child a pre-formed chenille star. Help the students glue the chenille wire on the illustrated star.
3. Say, **God helped the wise men find Jesus. God can help you find Jesus, too.** Talk about how the kids can find Jesus as their Savior today.

Visitors from Afar

They…worshipped him.
~ Matthew 2:11

Jesus' Family
Take the Safe Path

Memory Verse

Escape to Egypt.
~ Matthew 2:13

what to say

Joseph and Mary had traveled to the town of Bethlehem where Jesus was born. Over a year went by. When King Herod heard about Jesus, he did not like Him. God appeared to Joseph in a dream and told him to take Mary and Jesus to another country, called Egypt. Later, King Herod died and it was then safe for Joseph to take his family back home.

What You Need

❑ this page, duplicated
❑ crayons

What to Do

1. Help the students draw a line on the path to Egypt, where Joseph, Mary and Jesus will be safe.

2. Say, **King Herod didn't like Jesus because he thought Jesus would become the new king. God watched over them so the bad king would not find Jesus. God watches over you and keeps you safe, too.**

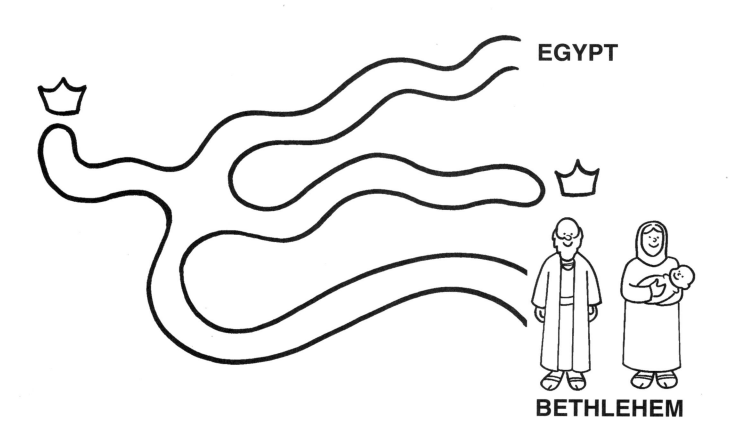

EGYPT

BETHLEHEM

Jesus' Family
Learning About God

Memory Verse

Jesus grew in wisdom.
~ Luke 2:52

what to say

Joseph, Mary and Jesus went to Jerusalem for the Feast of the Passover. Jesus was 12 years old. When the feast was over, Joseph and Mary began to walk back home to Galilee. Their friends and relatives were walking with them. After walking all day, His parents noticed Jesus wasn't with the group. They got worried and walked back to Jerusalem to look for Him. They found Jesus in the temple listening to the teachers and asking questions.

What You Need

- [ ] this page, duplicated
- [ ] crayons
- [ ] Bible stickers

What to Do

1. Have the children color the picture of the Sunday school class.

2. Give each child a Bible sticker to put in the teacher's hands.

3. Say, **Jesus wanted to know about God, so He went to the temple to learn from the teachers. You can learn about God and Jesus from the Bible, by going to Sunday school and by going to church. God is happy when boys and girls want to know Him better.**

Jesus' Family
Mud in His Eyes

Memory Verse

This man [has not] sinned.
~ John 9:3

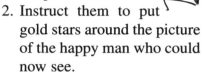 **what to say**

When Jesus was 30 years old, He began walking to other towns. He saw people who couldn't see or walk, and many who were ill. He began to heal them. One man was blind. The people wanted to know why he was blind. They thought he had done something wrong and that was why he was blind. Jesus told the people that the man had done nothing wrong. Then Jesus put special mud on the man's eyes. When the blind man washed away the mud, he could see!

What You Need

- ❑ this page, duplicated
- ❑ crayons
- ❑ gold star stickers

What to Do

1. Have the students color the picture.
2. Instruct them to put gold stars around the picture of the happy man who could now see.
3. Say, **Jesus healed the man because He loved him. Jesus cares for and loves you.** Using each child's name, say: "_____, Jesus loves you."

Zechariah's Family
My Hands Can Talk

Memory Verse

You will be silent.
~ Luke 1:20

what to say

Zechariah and Elizabeth prayed for years to have a child. One day when Zechariah was in the temple, an angel named Gabriel appeared to him. He told Zechariah that his wife, Elizabeth, would have a baby. At first, Zechariah didn't believe Gabriel. Because he didn't believe, Gabriel told Zechariah he wouldn't be able to talk until Elizabeth gave birth. Later, Elizabeth gave birth to a boy and named him John. Zechariah was then able to talk. He praised God!

What You Need

- ❏ this page, duplicated
- ❏ crayons

What to Do

1. Help the students draw a line between the person trying to talk with his or her hands and what he or she is saying (read the sentences to them).

2. Say, **It is easier to talk with our mouths than our hands.** Show how we can talk with our hands by rubbing our eyes to mean we are tired, or clapping our hands to mean we approve.

I AM SAD

I LOVE YOU

I AM HAPPY

Zechariah's Family
New Baby for Old Parents

Memory Verse

His name is John.
~ Luke 1:63

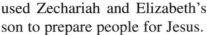 **what to say**

Elizabeth and Zechariah were married for many years but had no children. Elizabeth was old. One day, an angel told Zechariah his wife would have a baby and they were to name him John. The angel also told him that when John became a man, he would bring God's people back to the Lord. God used Zechariah and Elizabeth's son to prepare people for Jesus.

What You Need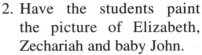

- ❑ this page, duplicated
- ❑ paint smocks
- ❑ paint
- ❑ paintbrushes
- ❑ water
- ❑ paper towels

What to Do

1. Dress the children in smocks to protect their clothing.

2. Have the students paint the picture of Elizabeth, Zechariah and baby John.

3. Say, **Zechariah and Elizabeth were both surprised and pleased to become parents when they were old. Your parents were happy when you were born, too!** Talk about all the special preparations parents make for a new baby and how happy they are.

Zechariah's Family
The Man in Strange Clothes

Memory Verse

Jesus was baptized.
~ Matthew 3:16

Before Class

Trace John's robe and cut out one from imitation fur for each child.

 **what to say**

When John became an adult, he lived in the desert. His clothes were made from camel's hair and he wore a leather belt around his waist. John's job from God was to prepare people for Jesus. He told the people they needed to be sorry for their sins. Then John baptized them. One day, John baptized a very special person — Jesus! God was pleased.

What You Need

❑ this page, duplicated
❑ imitation fur or felt
❑ small leather strips
❑ scissors
❑ glue

What to Do

1. Cut the fur or felt to fit John's robe. Help the students glue the robe on John.
2. Give each child a strip of leather to glue on the robe as a belt.
3. Say, **Feel John's clothes. Do they feel like your clothes? John told people to be sorry for their sins. God is happy when people say they are sorry for sinning. You can tell God you are sorry when you pray to Him.**

Zechariah's Family
Truth Preached in Jail

Memory Verse

Herod feared John.
~ Mark 6:20

Before Class

Each child will need four 6" chenille wires.

what to say

John told people to prepare for Jesus by being sorry for their sins. One day, John told King Herod that he was a sinner. King Herod got mad and had John arrested. While John was in jail, King Herod liked to listen to him preach. He knew John was a holy man. King Herod became afraid because he had put John in jail.

What You Need

- ❑ this page, duplicated
- ❑ crayons
- ❑ glue
- ❑ chenille wire

What to Do

1. Have the students color the picture of John.
2. Drop glue on each child's paper and help them place the chenille wires to make the jail bars.
3. Say, **Even though John knew he could go to jail, he spoke the truth to King Herod. It is always right to tell the truth.**

Mary, Martha and Lazarus
Mary and Martha Puppets

Memory Verse

*Mary…sat at the
Lord's feet.*
~ Luke 10:39

what to say

Jesus and His disciples walked around preaching to people. One day, they visited a town where Martha and Mary lived. Martha and Mary were sisters. Martha invited Jesus and His disciples for dinner. While Martha was busy cooking the dinner, Mary sat at Jesus' feet. This made Martha mad. She told Jesus to tell Mary to help her.

Jesus told Martha not to worry so much. Mary was doing what was good by listening to Jesus.

What You Need

- ❏ page 86, duplicated
- ❏ crayons
- ❏ 6" craft sticks
- ❏ glue sticks

What to Do

1. Allow the students to color Mary and Martha.
2. Cut out the puppets for the children.
3. Help them glue Mary to one side of a craft stick (half way down) and Martha to the other side (half way down). Then they should glue Mary and Martha together.
4. Ask, **Who will you be like? Martha, who was too busy to listen to Jesus? Or Mary, who took the time to listen to Jesus?** Have the students show you the side of the puppet for whom they want to be. Say, **Jesus wants us to take the time to listen to Him.** Talk about how they can sit quietly in Sunday school while listening to you talk about Jesus.

GLUE TO STICK

MARY   **MARTHA**

Mary, Martha and Lazarus
Moving the Stone

Memory Verse

It is for God's glory.
~ John 11:4

Before Class

Trace the patterns on page 88. Cut out one stone, one tomb and one Lazarus per child.

what to say

One day, Lazarus, Mary and Martha's brother, became very sick. The sisters knew Jesus had healed people. They sent word to Jesus that their brother was sick. Jesus waited. Lazarus died. When Jesus arrived, Martha and Mary were sad. Jesus told Martha her brother would come alive again. Jesus went to the tomb where Lazarus was buried. The stone was rolled away from the opening. Jesus said, "Lazarus, come out." Lazarus walked out of the tomb. He was alive!

What You Need

- [ ] page 88, duplicated
- [ ] gray and brown construction paper
- [ ] scissors
- [ ] glue sticks
- [ ] 9" paper plates

What to Do

1. Give each student a stone, tomb and Lazarus.
2. Show how to glue the tomb in the center of the paper plate.
3. Show how to glue Lazarus in the opening of the tomb.
4. Help the students glue one side of the stone to the tomb as shown so it flaps open. Write the memory verse on each child's plate.
5. Say, **When the stone is opened, we see that Lazarus is alive! Jesus raised Lazarus from the dead so people would praise God for the miracle.**

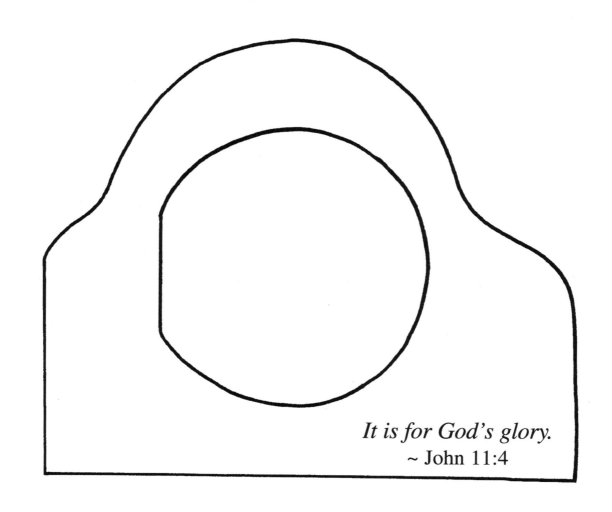

It is for God's glory.
~ John 11:4

Mary, Martha and Lazarus
A Medal of Honor

Memory Verse

She poured it on Jesus' feet.
~ John 12:3

Before Class

Trace the medal on poster board and cut one for each child.

 **what to say**

One day, Jesus came to the home of Lazarus, Martha and Mary. Martha cooked a special meal to honor Jesus. She remembered that Jesus had raised her brother from the dead. Mary had a jar of expensive perfume. She had worked a whole year just to buy it! Quietly, she poured the perfume on Jesus' feet. Then she wiped His feet with her hair. Pouring perfume on Jesus was one way Mary showed honor to Jesus.

What You Need

- [ ] this page, duplicated
- [ ] poster board
- [ ] crayons
- [ ] glue sticks
- [ ] ribbon (¼" x 15")
- [ ] hole punch
- [ ] scissors

What to Do

1. Have the students color the Medal of Honor.
2. Cut out each child's medal and help them glue it to a poster board circle.
3. Punch a hole at the top of the medal and have the child help you string a ribbon through the hole.
4. Before the students leave, put their Medals of Honor on them. Say, **One way to honor Jesus is by showing love to your family and friends.** Talk about ways they can show love to others.

A Father and Two Sons
Foolish Man Becomes Wise

Memory Verse
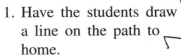

I have sinned.
~ Luke 15:18

Before Class
Trace a penny on gold paper and cut three coins for each child.

what to say

There once was a man who had two sons. The younger son wanted some of his father's money, so his father gave it to him. When the younger son left home, he began to spend all his money on foolish things. One day, he realized it was wrong to spend his money foolishly. He went home, asked his father to forgive him and offered to work for him. His father was happy to see him. He threw a party to celebrate his son's return.

What You Need
- ❏ this page, duplicated
- ❏ gold construction paper
- ❏ glue sticks
- ❏ crayons

What to Do
1. Have the students draw a line on the path to home.
2. Give each child three gold paper coins and help them glue them on the foolish man's path.
3. Talk with the students about how they can be foolish, such as eating all their candy at one time and having a tummy ache. Discuss ways to avoid being foolish.

A Father and Two Sons
Wise Man Party Time

Memory Verse

The older brother became angry.
~ Luke 15:28

 **what to say**

A man had two sons. The younger son foolishly spent his father's money. When he became wise, he went home to ask for forgiveness. The older brother heard music coming from the house. Their father was giving a party for his younger son. The older son was angry with his father. He didn't understand why his father would give a party for his foolish brother. The oldest son didn't go to the party.

What You Need

- [ ] this page, duplicated
- [ ] crayons

What to Do

1. Have the students color the picture of the older brother refusing to go to the party for his younger brother.
2. Say, **The older brother was mad because his father didn't give him a party for staying home and working hard. God wants us to forgive others and not be mad at them.** Talk about how God wants us to be forgiving and not angry.

A Father and Two Sons
Lost But Found

Bible Story
The father's explanation.
(Luke 15:11-32)

Memory Verse

We had to...be glad.
~ Luke 15:32

Before Class

Cut two pieces of paper (3"x 4") for each child. Print LOST on one paper and FOUND on the other.

what to say

A father had two sons. The youngest son left home and spent his inheritance on foolish things. When the youngest son left home, he got caught up in the foolish things of the world. His father was sad. But the youngest son soon found wisdom and returned home. Now his father was happy because his youngest son had been lost but now was found!

What You Need

- ❏ this page, duplicated
- ❏ crayons
- ❏ tape

What to Do

1. Have the students color each picture.
2. Give the students the Lost and Found sheets to tape over each picture.
3. Explain that when the students uncover the picture, they will see the youngest son lost because he was foolish, or found because he became wise.
4. Say, **You can be wise by believing in Jesus.**

Family of God
Circle the Sin

Memory Verse

All have sinned.
~ Romans 3:23

what to say

Adam and Eve, the first family, sinned against God. They ate from the tree when God told them not to eat from it. Sin is doing something bad. Hitting, pushing and disobeying to your parents and teachers are all sins. Everyone sins, but God wants us to do good things. God loves us and wants to forgive us when we do bad things, if we ask Him.

What You Need

☐ this page, duplicated
☐ crayons

What to Do

1. Have the students color the pictures of boys and girls doing good and bad things.

2. Talk about what the sin is in each picture. Emphasize that they are good children who sometimes do bad things (sin). Talk about the good things the children are doing in the other two pictures. Instruct the students to circle the pictures of children doing something bad.

3. Say, **God loves you and will forgive you when you do something bad.**

Hitting   **Pulling a dog's tail**

Picking up toys

"Yes, Mom"

Obeying Mom or Dad

Family of God
The Foot of the Cross

Memory Verse

Christ died for us.
~ Romans 5:8

what to say

Everyone sins. To "sin" means to do something bad, like hitting or pushing. We can do good things like sharing and taking turns. God loves us very much and wants everyone to go to heaven. God provided a special way for us to go to heaven. When Jesus died on the cross for our sins, He took away all our sins! All we have to do is ask for forgiveness.

What You Need

- ❏ this page, duplicated
- ❏ crayons

What to Do

1. Have the students color the cross.

2. Read the phrases below aloud and help the children draw an "X" on the sins to show only Jesus can take away sins. Explain what each sin is and then say, **Jesus takes away all our sins.**

3. Say, **You can give your sins to Jesus.** Emphasize how much Jesus loves them and wants to take away their sins.

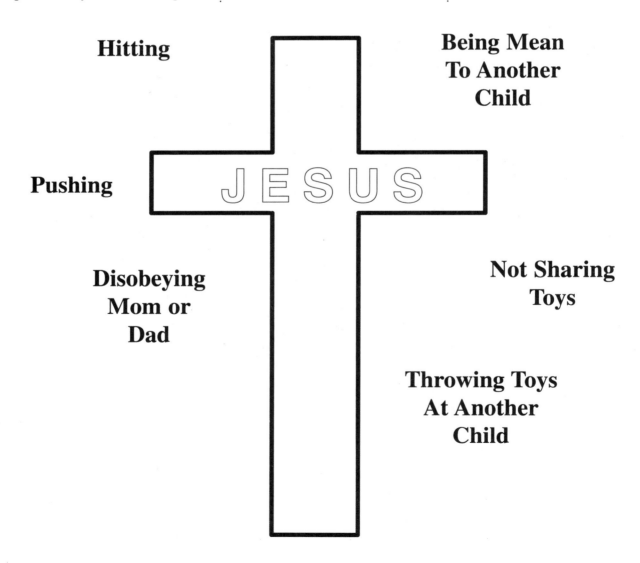

Hitting

Being Mean To Another Child

JESUS

Pushing

Disobeying Mom or Dad

Not Sharing Toys

Throwing Toys At Another Child

I'm Sorry, God

Memory Verse

He...will forgive us.
~ 1 John 1:9

Before Class

Make circles from colored paper using a hole punch.

 what to say

God wants us all to go to heaven to live with Him forever! The only thing that can keep us from going to heaven is sin. Sin is when we do something bad. When we do something bad, we need to pray and tell God about it. When we ask God to forgive us, He always does. God loves us very much!

What You Need

- ❏ this page, duplicated
- ❏ crayons
- ❏ glue sticks
- ❏ colored paper
- ❏ hole punch

What to Do

1. Have the students color the picture of the children praying to God. Say, **They are telling Him about their sins.**
2. Help the students put glue on the letters and colored circles on the glue.
3. Say, **God loves you and will forgive you when you do something bad.**

Family of God
Hearts for Jesus

Memory Verse

Whoever believes in him shall...have life.
~ John 3:16

what to say

God loves us and He wants us to live in heaven with Him forever! Jesus died on the cross for our sins. When we sin, we can tell God and He forgives us. God says in the Bible that if we know that we are sinners, confess our sins to Him and believe in Him, we can live in heaven with Him forever!

What You Need

- ❏ this page, duplicated
- ❏ crayons
- ❏ small heart stickers

What to Do

1. Have the students color the picture of Jesus.
2. Give the students some heart stickers to make a picture frame around Him.
3. Say, **Jesus loves you very much! You can tell Jesus how much you love Him when you pray.**